Dance Script With Electric Ballerina

Dance Script

ALICE FULTON

With Electric Ballerina

UNIVERSITY OF PENNSYLVANIA PRESS

PHILADELPHIA
1983

Copyright © 1983 by the University of Pennsylvania Press

Library of Congress Cataloging in Publication Data

Fulton, Alice, 1952–
Dance script with electric ballerina.

I. Title.
PS3556.U515D3 1983   811'.54   83-10319
ISBN 0-8122-7901-8
ISBN 0-8122-1155-3 (pbk.)

Printed in the United States of America

For Hank

Contents

Acknowledgments   ix

Introduction by W. D. Snodgrass   xi
In The Beginning   3

I

From Our Mary To Me   7
The Gone Years   10
Toward Clairvoyance   11
The Death Of Birds   13
The Perpetual Light   14
The Great Aunts Of My Childhood   18

II

Two Cries & A Clutch   21
Agoraphobia   23
Forcing White Lilacs   25
The Bundled-Well-Hung-Up-Tight-Don't-Put-That-In-Your-Mouth-It's-
    Poisoned Blues   27
Classified   28
Bad Actor   30
Snow-Kiln   31
Anchors Of Light   33

III

Dance Script With Electric Ballerina   37
Agonist Of The Acceleration Lane   40
You Can't Rhumboogie In A Ball And Chain   41
How To Swing Those Obbligatos Around   43
My Diamond Stud   44
Your Card Read "Poet-Mechanic"   46
Rose Fever   47
Needfire, This Low Heaven   49

IV

Life Above The Permafrost   53
Between The Apple And The Stars   55
Picture Planes   57
Chance Music   64
Reeling Back The Saffron   66
What I Like   68
Second-Sight   69
Yours & Mine   70
Sympathetic Hexes   71
All Blankets Should Be White   74
Diminuendo   75

Acknowledgments

Ambit: "Two Cries & A Clutch"
American Scholar: "Between The Apple And The Stars"
Aspen Anthology: "Bad Actor," "Diminuendo"
Bellingham Review: "The Bundled-Well-Hung-Up-Tight-Don't-Put-That-In-Your-Mouth-It's-Poisoned Blues"
Beloit Poetry Journal: "My Diamond Stud"
Boxspring: "Forcing White Lilacs"
Confrontation: "Chance Music"
Dark Horse: "Classified"
Georgia Review: "Dance Script With Electric Ballerina"
Greenfield Review: "All Blankets Should Be White"
High Rock Review: "Snow-Kiln"
Intro 12: "Life Above The Permafrost"
The Little Magazine: "Agoraphobia"
Michigan Quarterly Review: "In The Beginning"
Ploughshares: "From Our Mary To Me"
Poet Lore: "Needfire, This Low Heaven"
Poetry: "What I Like"
Poetry Now: "Second-Sight," "Toward Clairvoyance"
The Runner: "Agonist Of The Acceleration Lane"
Shankpainter: "Rose Fever," "Yours & Mine"
Urthkin: "You Can't Rhumboogie In A Ball And Chain," first published under the title "Sestina For Janis Joplin"
Virginia Quarterly Review: "The Perpetual Light," "Reeling Back The Saffron"

Washout Review: "How To Swing Those Obbligatos Around," "Your Card Read 'Poet-Mechanic' "

"Anchors Of Light," "The Death Of Birds," "The Gone Years," and "The Great Aunts Of My Childhood" first appeared in the chapbook *Anchors of Light,* published by Swamp Press of Oneonta, New York, 1979.

"Sympathetic Hexes" first appeared in the anthology *The Wings, The Vines,* published by McBooks Press, Ithaca, New York, 1983, and distributed by The Crossing Press of Trumansburg, New York.

I wish to thank Mary Callahan Fulton, Cornell University, The MacDowell Colony, The Millay Colony, The *Washout Review* Poetry Workshop, and The Writers Community, whose support helped me to write the poems.

Introduction

In *How to Read,* Pound identifies three ways the language of poetry is charged or energized: *melopoeia, phanopoeia,* and *logopoeia.* He describes the last of these as "the dance of intellect among words." He deems it untranslatable and "the latest come, and perhaps most tricky and undependable mode." I would add that it is conspicuously lacking from recent American poetry—as from recent American criticism, thought, politics, American life generally. Just when American dance itself is enjoying such an illustrious resurgence, the American intellect has to show itself creaky, overweight, and downright lubberly. *Logorrhoea?*—it's an epidemic; *Logopoeia?*—where? Yet, just when many of us had written off the American intellect as extinct, probably mythical, here steps into our dark and cheerless vale Alice Fulton, scattering "brio and ballon" on every side, the veritable Lady of Logopoeia.

In the title poem of this book she describes her own poetry—as also her life—in dance terms and a dancer's "getup":

> feet bright and precise as eggbeaters,
> fingers quick as switch-
> blades and a miner's lamp for my tiara.
> You've seen kids on Independence Day, waving
> sparklers to sketch their initials on the night?
> Just so, I'd like to leave a residue
> of slash and glide, a trace-
> form on the riled air.

Her life seems to have been a succession of dances, dancers, performers, costume. She recalls her mother, Mary Callahan:

> . . . swishing
> her housedress in a mad can-can, her legs
> brazening the air, her exit a "So there!"
> flip of skirt, capework defiant as a toreador's,
> leaving me weak with laughter—
> . . . kicking like a worm in a jumping bean.

Earlier in the poem, the exuberant Mary had "lost her drawers on the Green / Island Bridge kicked them in the river tap-danced / at the recital. . . ." Now Mary sits with her daughter and her daughter's friend, who are doggedly starving themselves while fantasying about an absurd future of luxury and glamorous lust:

> . . . They are thumping
> their feet to imaginary drums and thinking
> if John Lennon loved them they'd be skinny
> though for that to happen they'd have to be.

As alter ego she chooses a different sort of performer, Janis Joplin, who wants "No Chiclet-toothed Baptist boyfriend"—and shows it in her "brass-assed language, slingbacks with jeweled heel," her voice like she'd "guzzled fiberglass," and, above all, the costume we see her in, sell her on: "It's your shade, this blood dress. . . ." "It's you."

How many of the poems are concerned with dress—the costume of dancers, which is so often the costume of lovers. For unwanted lovers we see her (or her poems' speakers) going to bed bundled into macintoshes, galoshes, oiled wool sweaters, "everything but skin." Or we see the costumes for incursions to love's underworld:

> He had shag hair & a boutique. . . .
> a gangster with patent leather shoes
> to shine under girls' skirts & a mother
> who called him sonny. . . .
> . . . I should have been
> the singer in tight champagne
> skin waiting for him to growl. . . .

This affair develops into a fox-trot "till a guy / he knew from Sing

Sing cut in." Elsewhere, another lover arrives in the guise of a "Poet-Mechanic" who reassembles half her language into trampolines and Harley-Davidsons, the other half into unmanageable acrobats and Hell's Angels. She is left with only the adjectives "all day primping singing choruses of popsongs." When she scolds them about their magnificent antecedents, she discovers that even

>   . . . "magnificent"
>   is in the bathroom
>   humming be-bop-a-lula.

Finally, she hopes that even the dead who once waited "with heavy patience for our arrival" will be so transformed that they will

>   . . . hotfoot it through the universe
>   like supple disco stars: their glamor sifting
>   into our rare, breathtaking dreams, our rarer prayers
>   mere twinges in their unimaginable limbs.

Yet even when dance/song/performance is not the immediate subject of Alice Fulton's poems, we are always engaged by her dance of intellect, the sense of linguistic virtuosity Old Ez described. There is a constant delight and dazzle in language textures, the ever-shifting shock and jolt of an electric surface. This makes me want to quote longer sections, lest by excerpting, I make her imagery, her diction, seem more predictable, more readily graspable than it actually is. Let me turn, however, to a few passages where she treats the sky, the passing day, the seasons:

>   the new moon's just a luminous
>   zilch. Under it, dawn's
>   first nude streak startles
>   like a bikini line.

When a man (a lover?) sends her a tape of his singing, her heart "flap[s] like a screen door in a tempest." Intoxicated, she notices

>   night just sliding by
>   gentle and majestic as a battleship
>   with cut engines.

xiii

Again, she thinks of that white winter sky with which she will have
the ultimate lover's union:

> a white sky that colors the world
> its shade through snow's dim-
> inuendo. . . .
> as if it too were being
> diminished, when the blank below
> matches the blank above
> and the whole horizon goes.

It may be that at times the fancy footwork obscures the overall
shape of the dance—which is to say, I suppose, that she has not
quite decided whether she is a poet of style, like cummings or
Berryman, or a poet of subject, like Hardy or Frost. If this *is* a fault,
I must say it's a loveable one, the kind most young poets could brag
about. How many have the hope, much less the choice, of being
either? On every side manuscripts appear, with high praise, exactly
like seven other volumes one has read that year; if you accidentally
dropped and scrambled all eight manuscripts, not even their authors
could tell. In place of real talent, energy, passion, one sees poem
after poem written to fit the fashion, the political or literary movement
of the week, the needs of 1,000 half-dead graduate students, the
obsession and power-hungry theories of critic A or B. Alice Fulton
once remarked that, victory or defeat, she hoped at least to be
counted among the lively ones. If my vote counts for anything, she
is a shoo-in.

Besides, there are plenty of poems with no such problem. Take
the love poems, both those razzy pieces about the lust game and
those several less showy pieces about a fulfilled and peaceful love.
In "My Diamond Stud," that personage, whom she encounters in a
roller-rink

> . . . wheel[s] up shedding
> sparks & say[s] "*Ecoutez*
> *bé-bé*. I'm a member
> of a famous folded trapeze
> act. My agility is legend, etc."
> keeping his jeweler's eye on
> my gold fillings.

They will tryst together in "travel-folder heaven" where he'll "swindle the black heart / between [her] thighs" and dress himself in leather:

> . . . He'd never
> let anything touch him
> that wasn't once alive.

In "Second Sight" she discovers something more durable:

> . . . After we kissed
> I wore my mouth like a neon bowtie for days. . . .

and finds that where such kisses once roused only a jukebox crooning like that of the adjectives fired up by her "Poet-Mechanic," this kiss remains in continuum:

> its second-sight like a candle's: clairvoyant
> tongue quickening the night.

Finally, in "All Blankets Should Be White" she contemplates a still longer, more enduring love, another lover's costume, a recollection of the union with the snowy sky mentioned above:

> I want to use white
> as a cover   to wear
> a white flag for a nightgown
> inviting you to cast angels
> in my drifts   strip
> and know you won't see
> the scars receding into skin
> and old bruises skulking back
> to the heart   which is not white.

Returning to Pound, we remember that he said of his persona, Hugh Selwyn Mauberley, that "His true Penelope was Flaubert." I shall think myself little poorer in my predilections in claiming that my true Pavlova shall be henceforward Fulton.

W. D. SNODGRASS

Dance Script With Electric Ballerina

In The Beginning

the swimming teacher said, "Go with it,
it will hold
you. Don't you know
you're naturally pneumatic?"
Since then everything has happened
this way. What a buoyant journey!
Here I am
sensitized to the least cheep and twinge
of other beings and especially to my own
twinges. I didn't create this pain-
ful grace. I didn't
banish the primitive.

This minute my small toes are shrinking
of their own accord. I have no say
whatsoever. Blame it on buoyancy,
without which, rambunctious and passive
as a beachball on the breakers, I
never would have bobbled here.
The wild green groans
by which I lived before language
now gesture and have at me
only in dreams. I wake seeing myself
as a bottle holding an inexplicable

ship. Who stuffed that soul-
ful ballast of sail down my throat?
Who trimmed the rigging, intricate as nerves,
and moored the skeletal mast?
Its construction is beyond me.
I'm only the go-between
gleaming round this unknowable
cargo, headed for a speck
on the sea's rim in the hope
it can contain a shore.

1.

From Our Mary To Me

As a child, Mary Callahan admired
storybook orphans:
Anne of Green Gables, Uncle Frank's Mary, transported
from mingy asylums to wide-hearted strangers
from skimpy wincey dresses to puff-sleeved splendors
from boiled turnips to chocolate sweeties.
And noticing that
all orphans had blue-black hair and eyes and skin
white as lace, she pictured them
as consumptive Spaniards
flaunting veils, roses, fans, Valentino's profile
and somehow confused
their juicy lives with Mary Daneher's: a rich girl
whose carbonado hair,
peaked complexion, yellow pink
orchid and blue smocked dresses with hand-stitched collars
lisle stockings and especially
patent-banded tan suede high shoes
and maid escort to St. Patrick's school
seemed orphanesque and prevented
our Mary from venturing near, much less daring
a till-death-do-us-true-blue-kin-
dred-spirit-ship the way girls did in books.

At night our Mary read tales that made her blood jump,
gazed through isinglass at the coalfire
and considered her own adventures: how she'd
crawled into the bull's pasture lost her drawers on the Green
Island Bridge kicked them in the river tap-danced
at the recital sat inside a freight car
talking to a tramp till it began to move
nearly taking her to Avonlea or Kalamazoo.

———————————

Mary Callahan, her daughter and her daughter's
friend are talking about love and wealth and Mary
Daneher. Our Mary says "I'd like to see her now
to see if she has any smocking on her."
The girls are memorizing every recipe in this month's *McCall's*
because they haven't eaten in three days
because they want to look thin in their minis and hipslingers.
They are starving in hopes
of having a yogic vision: a lost Beatle
drives up in a psychedelic Rolls and proposes
whimsical English sex. They are thumping
their feet to imaginary drums and thinking
if John Lennon loved them they'd be skinny
though for that to happen they'd have to be.

Hopeless! They are hopeless!
I see their faces pinched with wishing
and see them settling for the life they fight
or a worse life they haven't bothered to consider.
I don't know whether to love or fear them.
From here I'd never find my way back
to that fanatic state: upper New York
Troy Michigan Deadend Avenue '67
my mother saying "Cheer up, girls," swishing
her housedress in a mad can-can, her legs
brazening the air, her exit a "So there!"
flip of skirt, capework defiant as a toreador's,
leaving me weak with laughter—
the anemic daughter, stranger to her
than any waif or ne'er-do-well
sat next to on a train, leaving me
neither her optimism nor charm,
only imagination, kicking like a worm in a jumping bean.

The Gone Years

Night pockets the house
in a blue
muffle the color
of my father's Great Depression.
I see him move
over the snow, leaving
the snow unmoved.
The snow has no imagination.

My mother and I shuffle by
each other as if we were
the dead, speechless
breathers at windows done in black
oilcloth tacked down by stars.

"It's fair that his clothes be worn
out as he was." She irons them
for distant cousins, the tattersalls
sending up a hush
beneath her hands.

Through January's flannel
nights she turns old
stories over and over,
letting the gone
years hug her
with his long wool arms.

10

Toward Clairvoyance

"Dust is the only secret"

Emily Dickinson

You hold all our home truths, nil-colored one.
Silk lingerie and high-rag notebooks are pilfered
sooner or later to your dumb dimension.
My mother railed against you daily
with my dead father's undershirts
in hand. But nothing flusters your calm
quantum for long. You'll allow
the piano its shine and move to stifle
a brass candlestick. Still

I like to think there's a speck
in me that couldn't be conscripted
just as a wind or river holds
your residue yet is always
breath or wetness. Lackluster stuff,
our throats close in your midst—we go wheezing
toward clairvoyance. Other presences
reveal their reasons clearly
to the senses. But you are most discreet and least
exotic, slipping your scant
cataracts beneath our lids each night. I hear

11

a voice in you like voices hidden
under hands, low conversations seeping
through the door's warped jamb. And the dust
a hundred miles away is your verbatim. Dullard!
who never spawns or swats
a single life, whose only racket
is our comeuppance, you lie
in ambush like a future
fact: a flat world
waiting to be
round.

The Death Of Birds

"A bird in the house means a death in the house."

All birds are removers.
Old Romans rubbed vulture
grease, vulture gall
on limbs to pick them
clean of pain, and some say
death dreams wing
away when you eat the wild
carrot, chew the black
seeds of male peonies, plants
you must follow birds to find.

But who can prove
the death of birds?
I've seen them maimed
by wheels, by pellets,
but never the crow
in its whole soutane, rigid
on the snow, or doves, those
professional mourners, gone mute
as puff-paste shells. I hunt signs

the way my late aunt squinted
long in mirrors, that day
the wren flickered in
and out her living
room, its life
assured, she swore
by the soul
asleep in its beak.

13

The Perpetual Light

(to my mother)

These gates are forever open:
Trees, weeping dishevelments
of leaves, Victorian granite
extravagances and sticky

tombstone verse are overruled.
Instead, cinderblock discount outlets
merge with headstones, plain
as ranch houses. The pink and turquoise

all-weather wreaths cloy
like petit fours issued in a famine.
Form following function,
the place is dead.

Remember Daddy's taphephobia? Unsure
the dead could hold their breath
forever, he favored mausoleums: air
at all costs. Practicality left him

here, in one of a dozen graves
he bought—the extras for as-yet-unknown
but needy friends. Today you and I
leave the air-conditioned comfort

of the Olds and get lost
looking for his stone.
The power mower putters round, tidying up
the plot, undermining the mysterious

14

half-world we know exists
if only we could find it. Here
it's too easy to feel invincible
as the relics that outlast us:

gold-plated backscratchers, new
wingtip shoes, small planets
of string. As if the dead spent
their lives salvaging and survivors lived

to raffle off the too-steadfast
inanimates. Our family favored
brash plastics to perishable cut glass.
The closets are a ruckus

of color: sturdy permanent
press or furious jersey
that combusts on the retina
and never fades. In your day

it was different. Sundays
your mother packed a hamper
of sandwiches and the family trudged
uphill to the graves.

Then monuments were figurative.
Only James's stone squatted discreetly,
serviceable as the Callahan's
hard grief: you who never hit

the ground and howled, but squinted
when the dead were mentioned,
like people staring into sun,
recited a few slow anecdotes

and let it go. It was impossible
not to personify: the ash and willow
tore their hair in the breeze,
you chatted with the mighty

gray angels or played in their wings'
gloom: two dark palms pressed to earth.
The family picnicked on a cloth.
No one thought, I'm sure,

to use the white iron seats
that seem crocheted by fiery-fingered saints
with a saint's idea of ease.
Later you studied the glitter

in the dull or rosy stones, wondering
was it smidgins of the perpetual
light you prayed to shine upon them.
"The things we survived

or died from!" you exclaim.
"James to pneumonia, as you know.
Fran lay huddled on the sofa
for months with typhoid.

Her hair fell out in hanks
and she never touched milk again.
Mother said it was skunk oil
cured her. Sickness, I remember,

had a different smell then. After Azalea's
scarlet fever they fumigated the house.
Harriet breathed some into her lungs
and died at three. As for me,

the walls swelled and burst
when I had mumps. Mother
tied my head in a flannel sling.
I told her that the rain was them,

the dead, shooting pebbles to call me
out to play. When the fever broke I wanted
a charlotte russe. She took the trolley
to Hardigan's and bought me two.

Spongey ladyfingers, whipped cream
and a cherry. It tasted like life
to me." Today nurses spray the sickroom
with Glade. The ill malinger,

treating us to chocolates
they can't stomach. Gallant
as astronauts, they wink
under the electrodes.

There is no quarantine.
My father's daughter, I
have nyctophobia. I know
the Grand Union's 24-hour light

scours each no-nonsense stone. I know
I should feel something
like consoled. Oh, Ma
how the world has changed us!

And the dead . . . let's hope
they're different, too.
That they no longer wait with heavy patience
for our arrival at some ever-open gate,

but hotfoot it through the universe
like supple disco stars: their glamor sifting
into our rare, breathtaking dreams, our rarer prayers
mere twinges in their unimaginable limbs.

The Great Aunts Of My Childhood

Buns harden like pomanders
at their napes, their famous good
skin is smocked like cloth.
Stained glass wrings out the light
and the old tub claws the oilcloth.
Kit makes cups of bitter cocoa
or apricot juice that furs my throat.
Mame dies quietly in the bedroom.

She pressed the gold watch
into my hands, wanted me to take
her middle name at confirmation:
Zita, Saint of Pots and Pans;
but I chose Theresa, the Little Flower,
a face in the saint's book
like a nosegay. I chose this

blonde room sprouting jade
plants, electric necessities
and nights that turn
my nipples to cloves
till dawn pours in like washwater
to scrub the floors
with harsh yellow soap.

II.

Two Cries & A Clutch

This boy liked me once:
two cries & a clutch.
Young blood, thin as a pick
he broke my lips & woke my tongue.
His contrary motions roughed
the nubs of my spine. I sharpened
my heart on his.

Now he keeps another nymph
in his guitar case: venus
plucked & scrubbed. He needs it
very clean. I need something more
than twenty toes twisting
beneath a sheet.

His shaggy hair's gone
lean. Mine's gray
as filaments: I own
this forty-watt glow, this season—
my flesh melts down, I stick
to chairs & churn
the words. His music
goes & comes. Where is the knowing
we sewed up years ago?

When we rubbed in the wet
storeways of Graytown, U.S.A.
police cars smoothed by
in the groundsteam, rain
made a heart murmur: *mine*
one of us said to one of us.
We didn't speak to strangers then.

Agoraphobia

It takes six coats
of lipbalm to steady her
mouth. Two hours for her hair-
style, an insulation
rigid with combs.

Lists must be made, itemized
with aspirin, sleeping masks, and a map
crosshatched with contingency
trains and cracks
she must not step on.

Getting to the door is hardest.
The feet know where they are
taking her. Sliding the heavy
chain makes the heart chatter.

Then the first slice of light
drives its spike in her eye,
air cuffs her cheek, a riff-raff
of noise homesteads the ear.

And every night it's the same
dream: quiet
filling the room like a water
balloon. The walls are fur,
even the doors are blessed
with no knobs. One window breaks

the wall she keeps behind her
back. If she turns
she knows there will be people
showing their teeth, pawing
the air as if to shovel it aside,
as if to beckon.

Forcing White Lilacs

First   the cold
the being held
to the ground.
Then to see things
the police won't
use, how his eyes
are tortoise shell, cracked
shoes layered with blacking,
the cigar and sweat smell
in the clothes   he rips
while snow drives
into her skin.
Her fear flaps at him
like a bat's shrieks
rebounding from trees
and she already dreads
the time it will take
to forget   the deep wavy tread
in his hair.
He is a squeezed tube
spurting words that knife
and twine like eels
under ice. He is all flesh
that wants into
hers. She forces herself
to think of anything
else: the flakes
a veil of buds   above
his shoulder she can see

light years of stars
yet night has knit
a stocking for his face.
He could be anyone
in the mild scum
of moon   he leaves
a foam on her jeans
she thinks of white
lilacs white lilacs
the first time   thighs
like packed snow
a sibilance of pigeons:
her cries unwinding
from his ears.

The Bundled-Well-Hung-Up-Tight-Don't-Put-That-In-Your-Mouth-It's-Poisoned Blues

They were always too long or short,
too cold or stirred up
tight in her breakfast nook
maybe wired with bracelets
or loud with tattoos
& God he glistens when he moves! She held them
at arm's length, wondered what possessed
this one, narrow as a casket,
that one wearing boots with spurs, & sure
she didn't want this
stranger holding her like some fly ball,
a fast one that happened to come
his way, she knew
she shouldn't have to
wear so many clothes
to bed, even in winter:
an embarrassment of galoshes, cowardly
macintoshes, oiled wool
sweaters, everything but
skin. Skin lived someplace else
as she let each man free
one clasp, unfasten, maybe
a buckle, a sash.

Classified

When I first see him, he is whipping
a tree. It yields
sinews the calm white of cold cream.
"May I sit the mare?" in cord
breeches he must weigh 200 pounds.

The bit is an icicle
on the tongue. The horse sighs.
"Of course, the price depends
on the animal. You know
I am a superb rider." He cracks

Leather against her flanks.
The mare grinds her teeth, a rhythmic
crunch of steel, turns
on the forehand, shoulder in, flying
changes, shoulder out, moving
off the leg, well mannered

Under his heavy hands
till he makes her take the high fence
from a walk. Then her legs unfold
too slowly and she goes down,
awkward as a fawn. "Goddamn
mule!" His fists jab the air, the mare

Foams, lays back her ears.
"Tijuana taxi. Worth about 32 cents
a pound." His eyes are fired
with bloodsport. I can see

He keeps mean geese and scrimps
on dusty hay. His horses' legs
are lumpy with splints
and they wheeze like antique concertinas.
All animals are psychic.
Already the mare is practicing her limp.

Driving home, the car parts fields
like a zipper. I envy the fuzzy nap
of trees upon the hills, the way
only the leaves are veined.

I can foretell
the phone at four a.m., the voice
saying "Do you wear chaps? A hacking
jacket? I think we can do business.
You know I know your name."

Bad Actor

My mother says he's a bad actor
the minute the paper is signed,
blood test done, leadshank
chafing my left hand.
He rolls his eyes. Barbed wire
finds his legs as he grazes.
Stalls disintegrate. Overnight
he hogs the grain and groans
with colic, bites my thigh
as I buckle the sheet and bolts
at the word "whoa." A good mover,
the girls in velvet
hard hats agree. Except for that
odd half-moon marking
on his neck. Wrong
on a blood horse.
That's why she's drawn to him
my mother says. Bad actor
that's why that's why
no schooling can save him
as he unwinds on the highway
as he jumps the first truck
wipers parting red
crescents on the windshield.

Snow-Kiln

The skin prickles, outraged as a cactus
at this cold. Toes difficult to place
as perspective in an Escher print,
and the whole hide trying
to jitter over its ribs.

The fireplace is certainly
a cipher. Only
the rag rug's vibrant
as a heating coil. I want to spiral
tighter than that
rug, tighter than the entrails beneath
my navel. Outside

the new moon's just a luminous
zilch. Under it, dawn's
first nude streak startles
like a bikini line.
Soon the windows will speak the blue
nuzzle of spruce and night
wind away to zero. The cold, too,

knows a circular motion. They say
it nadirs then turns
cozy, lulling lost hikers
to sleep in its snow-kiln.
Cold always grants us what we crave—
if we are patient, if we wait
out the delays: heat, heat.
Steeped in drifts
of sleep.

Anchors Of Light

Somewhere rabbits fatten exactly
ten grams a day
reaching the height of tree stumps
while the building I live in rises
into stars. An old pine grows,
small as a hairbrush
beside the door,
where the wind's lisp
is a trespass
lost in engines.

Rush hour brays
as mute dusk slinks behind
the neon, sashays toward my window.
Over the reservoir the sun
casts anchors of light.
The trees' red
webbed paws detach and cling
to windshields.

Given a tongue, the night
might persuade me
to clutch its hem and waltz
the air. Instead, pin-
curled, teething on sheets,
I sleep.

Up North, the snow collects
its portraits of claws
and the varying hare
tweeds to white: only
its black eartips hold
down the field like stones.

III.

Dance Script With Electric Ballerina

Here I am on this ledge again,
my body's five rays singing,
limbering up for another fling
with gravity. It's true,
I've dispensed with some conventions.
If you expected sleeping
beauty sprouting from a rococo
doughnut of tulle, a figurine
fit to top a music box, you might want
your money back. I'll take a getup
functional as light:
feet bright and precise as eggbeaters,
fingers quick as switch-
blades and a miner's lamp for my tiara.
You've seen kids on Independence Day, waving
sparklers to sketch their initials on the night?
Just so, I'd like to leave a residue
of slash and glide, a trace-
form on the riled air.
Like an action painter, tossing form on space
instead of oil on cloth,
I'm out to disprove the limited
orbit of fingers, swing some double-jointed
miracles, train myself to hover above ground
longer than the pinch of time allowed.

This stingy escarpment leaves so little
room to move!
But perhaps that's for the best. Despite brave talk
of brio and ballon, spectators prefer
gestures that don't endanger
body and soul. Equilibrium
is so soothing—while any strain is a reminder
of the pain that leads to grace:
muscles clenched like teeth to the shin, swollen
hubs of shoulder, ankle, wrist, and knee,
toes brown as figs from the clobbering
of poundage. In this game, lightness is all.
Here's another trick. When passing the critics
turn sideways to expose less
surface. Think like a knife
against the whetstone sneers: *unsympathetic*
in several minds   flat and hollow
at the core   shabby   too
flaccid   polishes off her pirouettes with
too assertive
a flick   ragged barbaric hysterical
needs to improve
her landings   technique   bullies
the audience into paying
attention   in short
does not really get around   lacking
assurance authority fluency restraint roundness
of gesture   something
of the air and manner of those who are ballerinas
by right rather than
assumption: one will say
I'm mildly impressed
by her good line and high extensions.

I can sense the movement
notators' strobe vision
picking the bones of flux into
positions. Can't they see the gulf
between gestures as a chance
to find clairvoyance—
a gift that thrives on fissures
between then and now and when?
If a complex network, a city, say
could be filmed for a millennium
and the footage shown
so in three hours it woke
from huts to wired shining,
its compressed assembling would be like this
dance: these air patterns
where I distill the scribbling moves
that start at birth
and dissolve in death.

Till then I'm signing space
in leaps angular and brief
as an electrocardiograph's beat.
Now as I settle on an ending
posture: my chest heaves,
joints shift, eyes dart—
and even at a stand-
still, I'm dancing.

Agonist Of The Acceleration Lane

I was a ho-hum tourist
who'd seen it all: postcards
of the Alps, documentaries
on Eskimos, knew it all
like the palm
of someone else's hand.

Locked in the body's stammer house,
I imagined fat thickening
the blood like gravy,
another summer, my soft
yogurt flesh nailed to the sand.

Then I noticed runners, industrious
as windmills, blood vigorous
as chili, & began trailing
after like an imported pull toy
in my mukluks & lederhosen,
manacles clamped to both knees.

Now every night it's the rub-
down with abrading stones, anointments
of linament & heat. I'm a believer
bleating this belief:
name me agonist
of the acceleration lane,
alive in the stretch
& the resting of sinews.

You Can't Rhumboogie In A Ball And Chain

(for Janis Joplin)

You called the blues' loose black belly lover
and in Port Arthur they called you pig-face.
The way you chugged booze straight, without a glass,
your brass-assed language, slingbacks with jeweled heel,
proclaimed you no kin to their muzzled blood.
No Chiclet-toothed Baptist boyfriend for you.

Strung-out, street hustling showed men wouldn't buy you.
Once you clung to the legs of a lover,
let him drag you till your knees turned to blood,
mouth hardened to a thin scar on your face,
cracked under songs, screams, never left to heal.
Little Girl Blue, soul pressed against the glass.

That voice rasping like you'd guzzled fiberglass,
stronger than the four armed men behind you.
But a pale horse lured you, docile, to heel:
warm snow flanks pillowed you like a lover.
Men feared the black holes in your body and face,
knew what they put in would return as blood.

Craving fast food, cars, garish as fresh blood,
diners with flies and doughnuts under glass,
Formica bars and a surfer's gold face,
in nameless motels, after sign-off, you
let TV's blank bright stare play lover,
lay still, convinced its cobalt rays could heal.

41

Your songs that sound ground under some stud's heel,
swallowed and coughed up in a voice like blood:
translation unavailable, lover!
No prince could shoe you in unyielding glass,
stories of exploding pumpkins bored you
who flaunted tattooed breast and hungry face.

That night needing a sweet-legged sugar's face,
a hot, sky-eyed Southern comfort to heal
the hurt of senior proms for all but you,
plain Janis Lyn, self-hatred laced your blood.
You knew they worshiped drained works, emptied glass,
legend's last gangbang the wildest lover.

Like clerks we face your image in the glass,
suggest lovers, as accessories, heels.
"It's your shade, this blood dress," we say. "It's you."

How To Swing Those Obbligatos Around

He had shag hair & a boutique.
In the bar he told me I had too much class
to be a telephone operator & I told him
he should have been thirty in 1940:
a gangster with patent leather shoes
to shine under girls' skirts & a mother
who called him sonny. He should have
crashed a club where they catered
to the smart set, disposing of
the bouncer with   You spent three months
in a plaster cast the last time
you tangled with me   & I should have been
the singer in tight champagne
skin waiting for him to growl
I don't know how to begin
this beguine but you certainly know how to
swing those obbligatos around & we
would fox-trot till a guy
he knew from Sing Sing cut in.
& he said he loved old flicks
I should come up to his place & see
the art deco ashtrays on his shag rug
that I shouldn't waste myself
at Bell tel but marry him
& take his business calls &
I said   How many years do you get
if they give you life.

My Diamond Stud

He'll be a former cat burglar
because I have baubles
to lose. I'll know him
by the black
carnation he's tossing:
heads, he takes me,
stems, the same. Yes,
he'll be a hitchhiker at this
roller-rink I frequent, my diamond
stud who'll wheel up shedding
sparks & say "*Ecoutez*
bé-bé. I'm a member
of a famous folded trapeze
act. My agility is legend, etc."
keeping his jeweler's eye on
my gold fillings. He'll know
what I really want: whipping
me with flowers, his fingers' grosgrain
sanded smooth, raw
to my every move. For our tryst
we'll go to travel-folder heaven
& buff-puff each other's
calluses in valentine tubs.
He'll swindle the black heart
between my thighs
dress me up in Ultra-
suede sheaths, himself
in Naugahyde. No,

leather. He'd never
let anything touch him
that wasn't once alive.

Your Card Read "Poet-Mechanic"

the day you came   carrying a two-cylinder
slice of winter sun on your back,
toolcase with a greasy lock in
your spoon-shaped fingers
said you could do anything
with your hands &
went right to work, using
nouns as furniture, assembling
verbs into go-carts & motorcycles
till they roared off, followed by
a gang of sycophant adverbs.
The few transitives that remained
you turned into trampolines &
the expletives jumped on them all day.
When I watched you build "vituperate"
into a Harley-Davidson, I knew
it was goodbye.
Now there're just the adjectives
all day primping   singing choruses of popsongs.
I want to shake them & say
"Have you no respect
for the magnificent
lexicon you represent?" But "magnificent"
is in the bathroom
humming be-bop-a-lula.

Rose Fever

Believing even an infant's primrose
pout devours what's sweet
and smaller than itself,
how can I surrender
to your embouchure
rippling all my pores?
Beneath raw silk, my thighs
tighten to a secretive frieze.

In restaurants you gargle
the champagne, all antics
and no manners, going home
dawdle on corners looking for cripples
to boost across: good,
too good. I know you
swiped these 12 long-stems
from some blind vendor. You're a knave
of hearts & now you've got me

crooning across dining rooms
and avenues, sniffing out
your soul where it dapples through
the shy skin circling your navel.
The solstice lengthens to a sexual pink,
pavement swoons between its curbs:

all my dark parts
itch with rose fever.
In a limp rally, I learn
the world's catcalls
by rote, thinking to note them
in your spell. See, I'm sound
in body but weak in belief,
caught in this airtight intersection
wanting to give in, gasping.

Lend me your gift
for plunder so I can blaze a way
through the shrapnel and the rapture.
Open your eyes and let me see
the innocent within,
his palms extended like a sharing.
Just slip me one unstudied look
before the retina sounds
its blue alert.

Needfire, This Low Heaven

(for Jon Randel)

Noticing a snow-filled shopping cart
outside the window
today, I imagined gladness
as its lack of hearty cardboards barking
100% promises: LIFE TOTAL MOST.
Forty-some superficial
muscles braced my inexpressive face
the way a fine steel mesh
sets safety glass, protects
a mildewed barracks partitioned into baffle
walls and lockers.

I picked up the mail mechanically
noting letters and a reel of music; began
threading the spool's dull ribbon through
sound heads, jiggling switches
till the tape pinwheeled, your voice
in it like wind, twirling song
from its frail rind. Then

entire projects of cinderblock suspicion smoked down
to a talcum, this one-cell
amoeba interior broke out in cabbage
roses. My heart flapped like a screen door
in a tempest. "Ooo . . . "
your low melisma lattices my spine
with vining light: "Needfire"
I'm naming this
eventful state, whatever low heaven
of rock & roll you send me
to. Now intoxicated to pitch

fatigue by all this
brilliance, I notice
night just sliding by
gentle and majestic as a battleship
with cut engines.
And through the open window
ice yields as mud
hums up, charging
the sockets of flowers.

IV.

Life Above The Permafrost

All winter the trees tossed in their coma.
Beneath them fields unrolled
like a pallet. Snow came,
the universal donor, the connective
in all the ready metaphors:
sky coarse as hotel linen,
bedsheets the half-white of rice
paper. That kinship.

Prone as the land,
I wanted each day to start
the way the body starts in sleep: a reflex
of sun, mimosa explosions. Not
the window's slow tap of sky,
light rising like sap
in maples, and even the maples
warted with sparrows
too frigid to fly South.
Those trees needed wild flamingos, at least,
to break their drowse.

In bed, my nails raked
the chenille spread, its whitework
like a mulch of snow. Snug as a corm
in its coldframe, the heart
shied from my five-fingered tongs.

Now there are parasol garnishes
on the rum drinks of summer, Adirondack
chairs with wind in the slats. Your arms band
me like a migratory bird. I think,
this must be life
above the permafrost. The raised candle-
wicking of the quilt
cornrows our skin. Our fingers braid
like aerial roots.

You make me want
to stop tending relics in my head,
that well-stocked potter's field:
just listen to the insects'
adenoidal plainsong all day long,
enamored of the keynote, the tonic.

Between The Apple And The Stars

"Newton did not shew the cause of the apple falling, but he shewed a similitude between the apple and the stars."

Sir D'Arcy Wentworth Thompson

By now we know
the portents: an apple falls
in a plague year,
a star rises
in the East.
A premature birth,

Christmas 1642.
"Small enough
to fit in a quart mug,"
his mother said. So feeble
he needed a brace
to raise his head.

Once after studying the sun
it took three days
of darkness to revive
his eyes. Then for months
when he thought *sun*
its ghost rose
on his retina.

But more than laws,
he sought the divine.
One Stone
to undo the skimpy differences
in matter: bread to flesh,
wine to blood, percolating wild
elixirs; even at the end
longing for "another shake
at the moon, another touch
at metals." Now gravity

lies passive as quicksand
under the jet.
But what of the Stone
with its "beravishing
smells, apparitions
of angels?" The scientist passes
a hand like a wand over
the wondrous button. The Stone

one day will render
all vibrancies
singular
as light. So apples
float from trees
and stars ripen
and die at ground
speed.

Picture Planes

I. Impositions on the Third Dimension

Long strips of curried animal
   skin beaded in intricate
      repeats of glass and bone trim
Cheyenne leggings. When worn
   the rhythm disintegrates
      to a hit/miss
fringe on the outer calf.

Another tribe makes monochrome
   mats of varying weaves.
      The pattern winks briefly
in reflective light
   then loses both sheen
      and motif. The artist's thrill
lies in its secret

scheme. It's that way so often
   to see anything we must attend
      a temperamental light,
squint, twist our heads, analyze
and finally shred
the whole to what
it was before the art imposed.

Finding the plane, straight
line, spiral, circle
in any as-is landscape
    isn't easy. Alright, some rocks
cleave flat and dead
stems rigor into line, there's the whorling
of ordinary snails, the o-
ccasional shock of bubbles. But
    these perfected forms are rare.
It takes artists
to stomp mountains down
dirt-smooth, starch marble
into columns, petrify
the snake in coil, keep
a thin-skinned globe
    from joining the indifferent

air. Nature's symmetry stands
uncertainly. Equality of trees
exists only in gardens or greeting
cards. Glimpses of scenery
    show a dissimilar twinning
often leaps east and west
of a vertical
axis: weed splits tree, tree
cracks hill, hill
guts sky. But it's we,
    the viewers, who have the bookend

look. Our own trunks break up
the wrestle of our arms,
two legs let us walk right-
left and some wisdom itches
in the bridge between our eyes.
    As long as we live we live
vertically, twilling the light
differently than rock, tree
or shark. We're the skipped strand
in the evolving
warp, classically
    stamping our double-fisted visions

on creation. For instance, painters
resent a form's excursions
in the third dimension, live to smear

slithery light and branching
shapes onto solid sheets, pillage
the world in a war so contained

it goes unnoticed. They'll take
a sea monster, say, and force its image
to a picture plane, intact. To do it

they must slice the thing in half.
A profile expels a hissing double
on the world, while a front view sets free

the flickering hinderparts. That's why
artists seek extremes: only the scaliest
dragon, snowiest angel will do.

Thinking of its dimensional soul, condemned
to wander, they leave cowed
monsters, fleeced seraphim.

59

II. His Acid Glory

Painting to a contract's explicit
stipulations: *"a procession with priests*
and other clerics solemnizing
the burial rites of Don Gonzolo, St. Augustine
taking him by the feet, St. Stephen
by the head, lifting him into the tomb, a great body
of onlookers witnessing and overall the heavens
opening out in glory" El Greco managed
to cram it all in-
to 15 x 11 feet. Nobody noticed
that he extricated the spine
and staked some gyrating
vertebrae in its place,
the way his figures'
feet stay glued to terra
firma as their limbs serenely cast off
gravity, thinning to the lank
sway of seaweed, or how the effort of suppressing
the third dimension vibrates
in their twist and torsion. That angels switch
like tadpoles through the heaven's membrane
and all his acid saints
are shaped like sharks.

III. Painting Masterpieces: A Fish Story

"My reputation is undisputed
in most circles." Domenikos
Theotokopoulos, a 440-year-old
Greek fisherman speaks from his bait shop
in Toledo, Spain. "It will be ages
before anyone matches it. My art is the art
of fishing for sharks
with party balloons, a roll of Lifesavers
and no boat.

60

Casting from land is out
since sharks cruise a quarter-mile
offshore, at least. So
I tied party balloons to the line,
let the ebb tide float it
into shark territory." Once there
however, Domenikos lost his bait
to insignificant sharks and never reached
the major monsters farther out
or deeper down. "That's where
the Lifesavers come in," he says.
"I thread baitline and balloon
string through the holes. The tackle
is in deep water when the candy melts
dropping the bait to the bottom
where the big ones live.

Of course, you have to be careful.
Once, to land an exhausted shark
I roped it and sat on its
back, so close I could see
the stigmata left by hooks it had outdone.
But my closest call came
with a giant stingray. From shore
I could see it leaping in high
relief like a struggling arch-
angel: dark gray wings
with that violet undertone. I waded in
to fight it and was pulled off
my feet. I can't swim but clutched
the line. Then a flying
buttress of a wave reared above me.
In a boat at its crest
sat Tiziano Vecellio and Michelangelo

Buonaroti who had been scuba-diving
nearby. They hauled me in and we took turns
trying to catch the thing, straining
to see the flake white belly
and spined tail whipping. Tiziano wanted
to harpoon it with his palette
knife. Then when it was almost dark
Buonaroti cut the cord.
A worthy man, Michelangelo,
but he never learned how to fish."

Domenikos's thrill of thrills?
The day he landed 30 sharks
on one hook. "I pulled
in a six-foot hammerhead with 29 miniatures
dripping from her sides like fringe."

IV. *Holding in a World*

All maps self-distort with the strain
of holding in a world:
architectural drawings let us see
around corners;
medical sketches show
the body as ocean—clear
container for an oddly bright

life. A deer with its heart roped
to its mouth by line
was the Pueblos' affirmation: hunger/pulse,
while South American tribes drew
white men with the all-important
mustache on the forehead
instead of stowed away
between mouth and nose.

Then there's El Greco
painting a world seen from a diving
bell, mixing aquatic
pigments for figures dripped
to unnatural lengths.
Square dalmatics of woven gold
anchor his clerics in lassitude
as Christ's grandeur sets
their wispy hands aflicker.

One critic lamented "the depraved
energy, morbid
forces" in the work. And there is that
welding of the suave
and stark, haggard
and ecstatic here and in all
things worth the wonder. A heaven and earth
suckled on the same light
as any Hades. The primitives
knew, El Greco knew

when a savior prances through
the traders topple
back like marble columns
in a bombed temple,
when a savior comes, drowned in sun-
beams, that black halo is a stingray's tail coiled but uncoiling.

Chance Music

You must love me
for what I'm not
or what could you mean
lassoing my vowels with catgut?
You have caged me
within a brace of staves, I have known
the mortification of calliopes,
onion flutes, ad libitum,
and Benjamin Franklin's glass harmonica,
that unnatural marriage
of wet disk and finger.

I say I have not been an accomplice.
18th-century Italians gelded boy sopranos
before their voices frayed, but I never
wished those small purses in barter
for high Cs. Witness
how I resist the violinist,
mewling under his plain-bow, forcing
him to détaché, ricochet,
and yet he claims to love me,
in my name takes trees, sheep,
stallions to make me sing
and I say I have not.

Listen. What I want
to say is not said
with Mantovani's vapors
or in crisp white Bach.
Let my enigmatic scale
sail through thrush, wind, street,
in an accidental way:
practicing dissonance
while the virtuoso sleeps.

Reeling Back The Saffron

Heat incubates: memories hatch
rapidly as fish roe. Hello to the gold
circle pins in blue Peter Pan
collars, the jaundiced
belly-up of Woolworth turtles
trapped in lacquered shells, the doll
with an up-do the color of cologne.
And hello sun: a touch-

stone caress continuous
as breath. In this weather
the lungs could bellow
their simple conviction
forever, reeling back the saffron
raft that held me, a morsel
above the lake's gullet, summer blood

sugar rising with the sweet
cream-filled cones. These nights,
banked between damp percale,
I face the odd fish
by my side & say hello.

He holds me as if I were
a small body, stocked with exotics,
where rainbow wrasse grew filmy
negligees in shallows
black as inner tubes, and leather
carp ground their teeth under
easy, opaque waves.

What I Like

Friend—the face I wallow toward
through a scrimmage of shut faces.
Arms like towropes to haul me home, aide-
memoire, my lost childhood docks, a bottled ark
in harbor. *Friend*—I can't forget
how even the word contains an *end*.
We circle each other in a scared bolero,
imagining stratagems: postures and imposters.
Cold convictions keep us solo. I ahem
and hedge my affections. Who'll blow the first kiss,
land it like the lifeforces we feel
tickling at each wrist? It should be easy
easy to take your hand, whisper down this distance
labeled hers or his: what I like about you is

Second-Sight

If I could fire a song so strong men cut themselves,
I won't say only when shaving, would you
be moved? Or say I dyed
my hair an alibi of sweet and twenty
would the odds improve? After we kissed
I wore my mouth like a neon bowtie for days, even
pleased with Times Square's holiday displays:
those electric devils pimping their winks.
Your voice sparks in me yet: a red signal leaping
up a radio tower, the stars chattering in light
years. One kiss, the kind that commonly dazzles
a jukebox to croon, but with me still in continuum,
its second-sight like a candle's: clairvoyant
tongue quickening the night.

Yours & Mine

Through your lens the sequoia swallowed me
like a dryad. The camera flashed & forgot.
I, on the other hand, must practice my absent-
mindedness, memory being awkward as a touch
that goes unloved. Lately your eyes have shut
down to a shade more durable than skin's. I know you
love distance, how it smooths. You choose an aerial view,
the city angled to abstraction, while I go for the close
exposures: poorly-mounted countenances along Broadway,
the pigweed cracking each hardscrabble backlot.
It's a matter of perspective: yours is to love me
from a block away & mine is to praise the grain-
iness that weaves expressively: your face.

Sympathetic Hexes

I've watched as one woman, adrift
and dizzied in the city's gridlock, circled
between Eighth and Broadway,
lobbed round by the crowd, waiting
to hit a win in her dreambook.
Racketeers print these books
where the beings and stuff of night
dreams are numbered.
But why play?
What makes the luckless keep faith
with their wonders
against all odds?
On West 55th I see the tight traffic open
before her blinkered stroll
and wish all sojourners a charmed passage
and night treasures.

———————

I know a few spells:
the way voodoo celebrants ring
little bells near the ear to ward off
possession. *Chevauche*, it's called.
"Mounted by Gods" who dance. The victim
is locked in drums, chants, smell
of blood and cigar smoke. Their Gods are Catholic
saints with African names.
A woman prays to Damballah—
Saint Patrick—in his cathedral,
while crosstown

young, streetsmart whores remember
just their first and last men.
They tell talky johns and hustlers
love is problems. A pimp says
She a gold charm working to keep me
nice in this place.
The way she tilt her hips make me
some real bank. With blue Lurex jeans
spread on she can make men
forget heaven.

———————

Heaven to the old hack horses
means a chance to stretch their necks,
check-reins slashed by kind vandals.
The local protection shop is looted, too,
and left ajar. Panic
devices and double-bolt tumblers
clench themselves with the petrified
rebellion of the gelded.

———————

Through air thick enough to lift
bridges, the Empire State sails:
a fluorescent schooner
above the wild undertow.
Nine million lives are deep in this
dreamcurdle where people succor,
murder, and forget themselves
who did it. There are nights I wake
to a woman's moaning
and don't know whether she calls
in love or suffering.
Her voice might be my own, your own, city
song the memory sails above the city's
din. But too often now the big ships'
vowels can't rouse me,
New York. Your rockabye's
the drug. Under its influence

I'd like to rip the bit
from a skittish red mare, dash bareback
past the locked botanicas on St. Nicholas Avenue
blissful and fickle as a voodoo saint
casting sympathetic hexes
on the redeemable dreams
of the dumbluck crowd.

All Blankets Should Be White

a mild insulation.
Grow old with white   patience
soon your hair will be riced with silver
face serene as a boiled almond.
Tell white lies
about the flesh that holds
your wagonload of bones
white and dying   to get out
like birches spiraled tight within white
tubes   the moon fisting its white
sliver through trees   this paper
spilling white noise:
I want to use white
as a cover   to wear
a white flag for a nightgown
inviting you to cast angels
in my drifts   strip
and know you won't see
the scars receding into skin
and old bruises skulking back
to the heart   which is not white.

Diminuendo

There is another sky
and then another, in smooth
segue. The windows are flush
with its thick fortissimo
or spacious blue,
with its one sun,
open as a whole note.

And all its moods just
suit me: the self-effacing
fall sky, gray and receptive
as tape to my voice, or luminous
in spring, with that glow
all gems borrow strictly from it.

Last night I heard a woman ask
a chance acquaintance, "Would you
hold me?" and thought
That's a question I'd trust
only to a lover
like the sky: too composed
for a quick or sour
motion. Its steady

glissando of light
never leaves anyone for long.
Maybe that's why
I like to lie under summer's
wide sun and I like this waiting

for another sky:
a white sky that colors the world
its shade through snow's diminuendo. A sky
that falls, touching me, at last
as if it too were being
diminished, when the blank below
matches the blank above
and the whole horizon goes.